UNDRESSED

Erica Loberg

chipmunkapublishing
the mental health publisher

Erica Loberg

All rights reserved, no part of this publication may be reproduced by any means, electronic, mechanical photocopying, documentary, film or in any other format without prior written permission of the publisher.

>Published by
>Chipmunkapublishing
>United Kingdom

http://www.chipmunkapublishing.com

Copyright © *Erica Loberg 2018*

ISBN   978-1-78382-439-7

UNDRESSED

For Wonky Women Everywhere

Erica Loberg

UNDRESSED

STATE PUFF MARSHMELLOW MAN

I hold my tears
Not cause I don't want to look like a sissy
Not cause it's a sign of weakness
Or because it makes people feel uncomfortable

I hold back my tears cause I don't want to wake up to a swollen
State puff marshmallow face
Lids that can't see in-between the inflamed lids of tears

That's why I hold back tears
I need to go to work tomorrow
I need to look presentable.

Commentary: Call it age, call it genes, call it what you want but, if I spend a night crying you better believe when I wake up my eyes will be swollen and look like marshmallows. I've tried freezing spoons and pressing them into my lids, which helps, but only time alieves the puffiness.

Erica Loberg

IT SAYS DON'T DRINK WITH ALCOHOL

It says don't drink with alcohol
And I toss it back on a dry falls
And it sits
Stubbornly
In the back
Of my throat.

And I re-pick up the beer
And take a deeper sip

To make sure it got down

Why do you have to dry out on my throat??!

Commentary: Sometimes I ignore the label on my medication when it says don't drink with alcohol, and in this particular poem I think I was stoned cause marijuana tends to dry out my throat. Well, it doesn't say don't take with marijuana on the bottle so that's ok!

UNDRESSED

THE JEAN SKIRT

I feel like my jean skirt looks like
Hannibal skin on a leg

It's that broken beaded thread

But

I can't seem to give it up.

Commentary: I had this jean skirt I bought in 2009. I rarely shop at all but got it at an American Eagle store at a mall near my work. It became my uniform. I wore it every weekend to the point that it became so worn and torn it had a rip across my ass, which would expose my underwear, so I'd have to make sure I didn't wear any of my loud colored undies. I had it for a decade, and then one day it was too much. It was so old I had to put it away, but, I didn't throw it out. I just put it in the closet somewhere.

Erica Loberg
JERK

"I wish I could just write."

She said.

I felt like a jerk

Like someone that didn't understand
Reason or logic

If you can write

You will never stop.

Commentary: People have asked me about my writing process. I don't have one. I don't sit at a blank screen and think what am I going to write about. It has always just come to me. I have no control over it, and it can be annoying. I can observe something, or feel something, and have an urge to write it down. I can't escape my need to write and this poem is a reflection on that, which can make me feel bad. It's almost like I take my ability to write for granted so when this particular women made that comment about wanting to write I felt like a jerk. People say I wish I was a writer, but unless you are, it's not a choice. The writer in you, has you by the balls.

UNDRESSED

THE HIGHER ROAD?

What's the higher road?

He fucked me over
And I'm supposed to take
The higher road?

When your name gets smeared across the flesh of outsiders.

I step on the elevator
And see one of his friends
Hiding from me

Head down

Discombobulated

Does he know the shame you have
Or should

And now carry?

Or did he tell you
Terrible things
About me
And now you're scared
Dismissive

So what am I supposed to do?

Pretend I don't know?
That we're stuck in an elevator?
With you pretending to not know me?
Me pretending that I don't know you're here?

And the doors open
For me to exit

And I turn my head to the side
And take a good look

Erica Loberg

I give a good look

At you

Despite what you've heard
About me
Bad, sad, crazy, depressed.

I'm here
It's me

It's me here now

So why are you hiding
And where is he hiding?

Commentary: When I broke up with my ex-boyfriend, he smeared my name all over town with everyone who knew us. In this poem I got on the elevator and one of his friends was already on it, and it was awkward. Why? Cause when I broke up with my ex, I kicked him out, and left the business. We were growing weed at the time and my ex hired someone else and this kid that he hired to replace me on the elevator tried to avoid me. Does this kid know he took over my half of the business and now thinks *I'm* the crazy one?! Am I supposed to take the higher road when I was the one who got screwed over? Fuck him and fuck that!

UNDRESSED

A WHIPPED HEART

And you whip my heart
Back and forth
And back and forth

But there has to be a forth for a back

So we're both guilty.

Commentary: I wrote this poem when I was in a tumultuous toxic relationship at the time, and this poem points to the back and forth, break up then get back together cycle that I endured in my relationship. Despite the fact the he was in the wrong most of the time, in the poem I take responsibility for going back. He may have hurt me but I stayed so we're both guilty of engaging in a terrible cycle.

Erica Loberg

CURRENTLY

I'm skinny, currently
Currently

What does that mean?
How long does
Current last?

Till next week
Next month
Next year
Yesterday?

When you dabble in and out of cheese
And wine and beer and this and that
Your currency

Flip
Flops

So there is a *current* skinny

But not a lasting one.

Commentary: I have always been a life size yoyo when it comes to my weight. I get skinny then think ok, I can eat now then get fat and think ok, I can't eat now, and it becomes this vicious cycle where I know I am going to either gain or lose weight so when I am skinny it is only "currently" cause gaining weight is just around the corner. Sucks.

UNDRESSED

DIM

It's interesting
Shocking
Unreal
        lost
        confusing
        slightly

When you look at your beloved
In the eyes
After a shattered
Glass
Of your heart

And still see the glisten
In the eyes

And yours have gone

Dim.

Commentary: One *tiny* detail that kept me in a bad relationship was my boyfriend's eyes. When I would confront him about cheating he would deny deny deny and would always have this glisten in his eyes that made me believe him. That made me stay, however, over time I became worn down. My eyes were dark with sadness, while his remained alive.

Erica Loberg

ALRIGHT THEN

I walk around my place
In underwear
And a shirt

Like I always do

And people get judged.

Then I watch Guns N Roses live
In Tokyo.

Axel's walking around the stage

In underwear.... Alright then.

Commentary: I'm not a full blown nudist but I don't like clothes. I don't like feeling confined, and when I am home, I'm usually in underwear and a shirt. People have judged me for that like it's not normal or weird. But it's ok for Axel Rose to pounce around stage in front of thousands of people with his tightly-whities on? Okayyy.

UNDRESSED

DRUG

You're like a drug
That I didn't
Know had me
Lost

I'd call you
Crave you
And get no response

I'd text you
Nothing

Then I became
Your drug

You shouldn't stop
Calling
Or texting

We are each other's
Drug

Commentary: It's all just a big fat game. For the most part, guys like the chase, they want what they can't have, and this poem points to that fact cause when I stopped pursuing this particular guy only then does he wants a piece of me. The tables turn. Stupid game.

Erica Loberg

IPhone

Every penis
Finds a hole
In the dark

But I can't find the hole
For my battery
To

Plug in my Iphone.

Commentary: I can never find the socket in the dark to plug in my phone, and always wonder how a dick can so easily find a vagina hole when it is covered by lips. The socket is out there with no obstruction yet, I can't find the hole?

UNDRESSED

DIPSHIT

Sometimes I think
Well maybe if I was a
Dipshit

Things might have been easier.

Commentary: I am someone that gets taken advantage of more so than most, and sometimes I wonder how my life would be different if I wasn't so nice.

Erica Loberg

THAT LIVING HURTS

It's dark
It's hard
It's not acceptable

That living hurts.

Commentary: Being a human being is not easy, and that's just the bottom line.

UNDRESSED

ONE IN THE SAME

You say you don't know
How to dance

But you know how to fuck

They're one in the same.

Commentary: In my opinion, if you can dance, you can fuck. Both require rhythm and coordination. I think you need to be coordinated to be a decent dancer, and if you're coordinated your probably better in bed and this poem draws on those similarities.

Erica Loberg

SHOE

It's almost like you're waiting

You're waiting for another shoe
To drop

But when there have been
So many shoes

What's another one?
And why am I waiting for it?

Commentary: The metaphor of a shoe dropping points to the array of hardships that have crossed my path in life. I question why I wait for something bad to happen when I know something bad is going to happen anyway.

UNDRESSED

Can't a woman get her two-buck chuck and some chocolate and call it a night?

I wanted chocolate and wine
So I threw on my trench coat
And flop flops

I felt fat and frankly didn't feel like dressing
Much

"I love your jacket."
What?
"Yeah where did you get it?"
Huh?

I was in line waiting to purchase my goods
At my local store

I was confused by all the attention

"It's old. It's from the 90's"
I said

And stuffed my hands in my pockets to better seal the buttons
Running down
To trap my shirt and underwear
Beneath

"And I love your gold toes."

I looked down thankful the attention wasn't on my clothes

I looked like a hippy pimp in flip-flops and a black trench coat

I was only a block away from home
And fleeted

Can't a woman get a two buck chuck and some chocolate and call it a night?

Erica Loberg

Commentary: I've already admitted I don't like to wear clothes, and when I am home I wear underwear and a shirt. Ok, this is lazy of me but, on this particular night, I didn't feel like getting dressed so threw on a long trench coat. I only had to go across the street from my building to the local CVS and of course I have to draw attention to myself. I guess I looked guilty or like I was hiding something, which I was - my half naked body.

UNDRESSED

OUCH!

Always shove up
Any peek a boo
Nose hair back
Up
Your nose.

Or pluck that stray away
Out.

Especially if it's spearing
Out of your nose
Like a toothpick.

Before

You thread your mustache

Or else

That thread might just yank
That bitch
Out

Ouch, shit!

Commentary: Waxing hurts, threading hurts, any ripping off of hair is painful. One day I went to get my moustache threaded, and I had this one nose hair that was sticking out of my nostril. When the lady got near the string plucked it out. It freakin hurt worse than threading all the moustache hairs so after that I made sure to always shove up any unwanted hairs up my nose to avoid that pain from occurring ever again.

Erica Loberg

DOUBLE FISTED

I don't understand people that brunch

With coffee
and a mimosa

It's like taking an antidepressant
with a shot of whiskey.

Commentary: I like to go to brunch on Sundays alone. I like to sit at the bar and talk to random people, or just observe the scene. This one particular day I was sitting next to this couple that were drinking coffee and champagne and it struck me how odd it was to mix the two - an upper and a downer. A simple observation results in a simple poem.

UNDRESSED

AND…. WHAT

When you whip your face
Left to right
With the back
Of your hand

You are ghettoing it.

Commentary: People might be offended by this poem cause I use the word "ghetto." I think it is no longer considered politically correct but at this moment I didn't have a napkin to whip my mouth so used the back of my hand. That is not "proper" etiquette aka "ghetto."

Erica Loberg

HARD BUBBLES IN THE THROAT aka PET THE FAT

Strength Strength
Strong

The hard liquid bubbles in the back of
the throat
make it hard
to swallow

That's what fear
mixed with nonsense
and the unknown

form
when you fight the cry

Sit up straight
pet your fat

and keep going.

Commentary: Crying is often considered a sign of weakness. Whenever you try to keep from crying it literally hurts in the back of your throat. In this particular poem I champion crying, and think it should be more acceptable. Whatever your troubles are cry it out, and keep it moving.

UNDRESSED

DR'S APPOINTMENT

You can't eat or drink after midnight
They tell me

Before the blood examine

Ok
I'm used to not eating.

Commentary: After six, it sticks! I find it funny when I am told by a nurse or doctor not to eat or drink after midnight if I have to draw blood or have surgery or something. The person always seems to deliver it like it is so hard or something. It's not. I try not to eat after six cause after six it sticks so not eating after midnight….no problem!

Erica Loberg

KNOCK KNOCK WHO'S THERE

And this is two minutes of my life

Knock
Knock
Knock

Who is knocking on my door?
I think

Is it my ex?
Shit, I'm wearing my "Working Girl" socks with sneakers
And not heels

In a quick second I contemplate
Putting on heels

Contemplation means at least a minute, and this is not the case
So that's not the right word but

I said ok, no heels, let's go

And I opened the door.

Heelless with socks on.

Commentary: After I dumped my boyfriend, sometimes he would come knocking on my door in the middle of the night and it would startle me. I would momentarily panic and think what should I wear? Do I put something sexy on to make him feel bad, or just wear whatever I have on? This poem reflects on that mere moment you go through trying to decide what to wear when you open the door to an ex. Just wear whatever you have on at the time ok. I think.

UNDRESSED

PLEASE GOD SEND HIM BACK

She sleeps alone
Beside her cat

He fills the void
She tries to crack

And when she thinks
She lost her man

She prays
Please God don't send him back.

Commentary: People deal with this all the time. They live with someone and share a bed and when it's over where do you sleep? In the middle of the bed? On your side of the bed? When my ex left his spot became occupied by my fat cat. He would lie there like a human being every night when I would go to sleep. It was comforting cause he replaced that void, but it also made me sad. I liked having my cat there but loved having a man there.

Erica Loberg

TO BLOCK OR NOT TO BLOCK

Is that the question?
Cause it's not an easy answer.

We fight
You block me
I find out
I block you

We make up
I unblock you

But did you ever find out
That you were blocked?

Commentary: I hate this shit. I actually wrote an article about blocking or not blocking a person's calls and had an outpour of comments by people dealing with the blocking game. I don't have an answer. If you want to block someone do it, if you don't, don't, but, if you block someone's email know that it is not gone forever. It's sitting in your junk folder. Don't ask me how I know that cause it is not good.

UNDRESSED

OBSSESSED

Obsessed

Every text
Is it him?
Every email
Is it her?
Every ring
Am I in?

Is she still pissed at me?
Did he stop loving me?

Obsessed.

Commentary: The modern age with social media, texts, emails, phone calls, all of it can drive someone crazy. The only way to not obsess is to take a break from all of it. Or else, it can get to be too much.

Erica Loberg

SHE STOPPED MY HEART

She stopped my heart

It started beating
Real fast

I tried to breath
But it wouldn't last

She waved goodbye
And it bled inside

I wasn't ready to die
But love is no lie

She stopped my heart

Commentary: Sometimes when I get bored with my writing, I rhyme. I'll also try something new and different like switching my perspective from female to male. The majority of my poetry does not rhyme but rhyming comes easy to me so when I feel like it I'll dabble in rhyming.

UNDRESSED

LIKE IT'S NORMAL

I wonder down the streets
Alone

I walk by bodies
Resting on the concrete

Like it's normal

Homeless is not normal
Normal is not homeless

But somewhere between being home-full
And becoming homeless

Without a home
Becomes a home.

Commentary: I live in Downtown LA and there are lots of chronic homelessness. It can be any time of day or night and you are bound to walk by a body lying on the sidewalk, and people just walk on by. It's sad that it is normal when it is not, but, if you are chronically homeless the streets become your home. I had a friend that was a social worker that helped to house the homeless in LA and he would tell me how hard it was to get homeless people to want housing. I didn't understand it then he said what would you think if knocked on your door and said "Wanna come live outside?" That story made me realize that asking someone if they want housing after years on the streets sounds just as foreign as asking someone who has housing if they want to live outside. So, what's normal?

Erica Loberg

A SWALLOWED HEART

I swallow my heart
In the back of my throat
To keep myself from crying

When you left
Me.

Commentary: Breakups are sad, and you should let yourself cry instead of stifling it cause it hurts, literally.

UNDRESSED

WRITING

I stop with a
Comma
Then on three
With a space
Here
over there
And people don't get it
every word counts
every pause.....dot dot dot.

Commentary: I pay a lot of homage to writing, poetry specifically. Poetry is my best friend, my eternal friend, till the day I die, and I write a lot about it. When you write poetry, for me more so than prose or other formats, every single word, punctuation, space, all of it matters. One line, one word, one comma can make or break a piece of work. Sounds crazy but about a decade ago I applied for a PHD in English and when I was conducting research for my admissions paper I came across this quote which has stayed with me ever since:

In the truly great poets… there is a reason assignable, not only for every word, but for the position of every word. Samuel Taylor Coleridge (1772 – 1834)

Erica Loberg

WHIRLING AROUND MY HEAD

This year is almost over
It has been hard for many

So I swirl my scarf
Around my head

Like a washing machine
Whirling around
My being

For one brief moment.

And feel better.

Commentary: I had a hard time in my 30's. My job situation was bad, my relationship at the time was bad, all of it was bad. One night I jumped up out of my desk chair and whirled a scarf above my head kinda like a wild mad person but it made me feel better. Even if it was just for a moment.

UNDRESSED

TURKEY BACON

Ah....terrible

I chew on
Turkey bacon

Like leather
On my tongue

And think I'm
Being "healthy."

Please.

There's nothing healthy
About that.

Commentary: Who doesn't like bacon, ok it's bad for you, it's disgusting when you think about it but we eat it. Then turkey bacon came along. When I go to Trader Joes I buy their microwave turkey bacon and think I am being "healthy." It tastes like cardboard cause I never seem to microwave it right and cause it is "healthy" I end up eating most of the bag. So, at the end of the day, what's the difference?

Erica Loberg

BARELY

I fall back
Onto the bed

Sucking in my
Parts

Beyond my stomach

Suck it in

And find the zipper to close the piece

Ok

Yes

I got this

I made this

My sisters hand me down jeans

Fit me

Barely

I can breath… I can breath…

barely

Commentary: We've all done it. We lie as flat as possible on the floor or on the bed and suck it in to get our jeans on. Even if you can barely breath and are in constant pain you do it, you wear it, you got it!

UNDRESSED

WITH LOVE

I walked into your heart
And you looked to the side
and saw the blood
filing your body

With love.

Commentary: I don't recall writing this poem but it makes me feel uncomfortable reading it now.

Erica Loberg

WAR AGAINST THE PENIS

That's what I said
After what felt like
Hours hours hours
But was really
Minutes Minutes Minutes

Giving the BJ

My arm was shaking from holding my body up while I
Was on my mission
Half way through
I realized
I was in for a feat
After what seemed to be forever
When I almost gave up
I thankfully tasted the pre cum
In my mouth
So knew
Ok
I'm almost done
But no
I'm not

"I'm holding out."
He said
What why?
I'm dying here!

A tongue is a hard muscle so I am not worried about it falling apart
But my neck hurt
My limbs were unsturrdy

It was war against the penis

Commentary: When I was in high school my friends and I formed what we called, "The Blow Job Club.' We would get together and discuss how to give the perfect blow job. I remember the one

UNDRESSED

major rule for giving a superb blow job: Commit. You got to commit. No matter how tired you get, or feel like you're failing and it's not working, you just keep going. You don't have to have the best form but you have to be fully committed to make it work.

Erica Loberg

WATER MEANS A LOT

So it's a different Christmas
Since 200...?

I'm not in a shower washing memories into my pores
I'm in a bath washing in sope avoiding memories

Newness
Fresh

Searching for a new bath
Without realizing it

I hear the changes of season
In the water

Whether it's streaming down in the shower a decade ago
Or encompassing my body now
The day brings light
Birth
Re-birth
Realization.

Water means a lot.

Commentary: About ten years ago I wrote this poem on Christmas that I thought of in the shower. It was called *In the Stream*. When my Dad died I stopped going to Christmas. This poem is a reflection on that.

UNDRESSED

AND IT'S AWESOME

This year sucked.

Depression.
Death.
Family

And everyone's world falls apart.

You search to find solace, truth
Something to keep walking
Then you realize you're not that special
Life is hard for everyone.

"Let it go, or be dragged."
I heard.

So I listen to Willie Nelson
On the Road Again

And it's awesome.

Commentary: I had a bad year after my father died. So much havoc unfolded in the family that every day was another nightmare. I had a hard time dealing and one day I was on the phone with a client that was talking about his schizophrenic brother. He talked about all the hard years he endured trying to help and manage him then said he came to the conclusion you either let go or be dragged. At the time my family was at war and I had a hard time managing and his quote stuck with me. Whenever I got caught up in the drama I thought ok I'm not going to be dragged down. I would listen to one of my father's favorite musicians and find solace.

Erica Loberg

ALLL DAYYY LONGGGG

why why why why why
will you not leave my mind?!

i've done everything to forget you
therapy, meditation, change my hair, buy new clothes…

and nothing

just more you you you
allll dayyy longgggg.

Commentary: I swear to God it has to be something worse than a co-dependency disorder. When I got out of my relationship with my Ex, it wasn't over. It never seemed to be over, at least not in my mind. I don't even know how many hours, minutes, seconds he crossed my mind every day. EVERY DAY. I always said given the chance I wouldn't change my brain but, when it comes to obsessive thinking it's terrible.

UNDRESSED

AFRAID

I'm not afraid to die
But I'm afraid to die alone

I'm not afraid of life
But I'm afraid of life alone

I'm not afraid of being afraid
But I'm afraid of being alone.

Commentary: When I broke up with my boyfriend who I thought I was going to marry, and my dad died shortly after, and my family fell apart, I realized I was on my own, and it was scary. I had no boyfriend, or husband, or family, and it scared me.

Erica Loberg

EVERY TIME

Knock knock knock
On my deaths door.

Every time you drink too much
Every time you fuck too much
Every time you continue to have
Another time

Every time.

Commentary: I have always had trouble with moderation. I have 'bouts of hard partying, with reckless sex, and just think I'm going to be ok. It's not going to ok every time.

UNDRESSED

I'M WHITE, AND I'M NOT SORRY

Is this about the color of my skin?
Or the zip code I live in?

I can't just sit here and take your mean girls mode
Just cause you've been a minority
The majority of your life

And white is the new minority
Is it payback time for old minorities?

Cause

I'm white, and I'm not sorry.

Commentary: I once had a job where I was the only white person. It wasn't just the Chola co-workers but my boss would say things like "You're white… you just have to wait for your parents to die and then get all their money." I would be subject to racism all the time and would just sit there and take it. Till one day I decided not anymore, I'm white, and I'm not sorry.

Erica Loberg

MY FAT

I pinched it
I pulled it
I grabbed it
I slapped it

For 30 years.

And when you died
I stopped

Pinching
Pulling
Grabbing
Slapping

I stopped the undying obsession with

My fat.

Commentary: When I was about ten years old I tore my patella tendon in my knee, and had to wear a brace for several months. I was always an active child so when I couldn't play I slowly developed a roll of fat on my stomach. Thirty years later, it was always been with me. But, when my dad died my therapist pointed out that I stopped talking about my weight. My father had always been critical of my body fat and when he died, I stopped caring without even realizing the impact he had on me, and my fat.

UNDRESSED

YOU STOPPED

I asked you to stop calling me
And you did

I asked you to stop emailing me
And you did

I asked you to stop texting me
And you did

So why am I so sad that you stopped?

Commentary: When I broke up with my ex it became a long break up. We would still see each other, sleep together occasionally, stupid. But he was always the one pursuing me, and it went on for YEARS. Then somehow one day out of nowhere he stopped, and I had the hardest time dealing and sadness took over for MONTHS. Be careful of what you ask for.

Erica Loberg

IN MY THROAT

I think
I left my heart
In my throat

When I left you.

Cause when I think of you
I feel it pounding
In my lungs

I find it hard to swallow
And then it starts to cry

I can feel it against the walls
Of my esophagus as it
Beats and beats and beats

In my throat.

Commentary: When I was a kid I would try really hard not to cry cause it would hurt my throat. Now when I cry I still feel the pain in my lungs but don't try to smother it. Gotta let that heart breath out of your mouth ok.

UNDRESSED

CAN I SEE YOUR BUSH?!

It was just a regular
Tuesday morning

When the agency mogul
Ran up to my desk

High on coke
And said,

"Can I see your bush?!"
"Ah, no."

And I just kept on writing.

Commentary: I've been sexually harassed my entire life. In this particular incident it was one of my first jobs out of college. I was working at a boutique literary agency in Beverly Hills as an assistant and this occurred. I posted it during the # Me Too campaign and one of my old bosses wrote a comment about being a redhead and how that gets people's attention. He also was a redhead and his comment made me laugh cause years ago he also harassed me. I guess he forgot.

Erica Loberg

UNLEASHED

In between seconds of time
I think of you

Alone in my mind
Alone with you

You remain unleashed
In my thoughts

Everywhere
All the time

And I don't know when
Or if

You'll ever escape me.

Commentary: This poem explores the idea that a person you love can remain stamped on the mind, and you might never be free. At least, not yet.

UNDRESSED

40

40 40 40 40 40
Is this what it is supposed to be?

Am I supposed to be alone?

Sans kids?
Sans husband?
Sans friends?
Sans knowledge of where I am going?
Sans understanding what I am doing?
Sans knowing why I am here?

I lost my dad
I lost my sister
I lost my boyfriend

And in doing all that

Have I lost myself
At

40?!

Commentary: The year my father died I had a real hard time adjusting to the world. I didn't have a safety net anymore, and it was scary. I was past the age of having kids and being 40 made me wonder what was going to become of me. I wasn't entering a midlife crisis, at least I don't think I was but somewhere deep inside me, I felt like I was in crisis mode, and had no idea how to make it end.

Erica Loberg

CAN ANYONE HEAR ME?

I have…

Over a thousand poems
Over five books
Over 800 blog articles
Over 100 YouTube videos

And

Nobody knows me
Nobody follows me
Nobody reads me
Nobody cares

…So can anyone hear me?

Commentary: Sometimes I get pissed. Sometimes I get confused. Sometimes I get down. Sometimes I feel like I am spinning endless wheels going nowhere, and it drives me mad. Sometimes I wonder if I am supposed to be a poet. Maybe I am not as good as I think I am but then I read something I wrote and I feel it in my bones. I feel it feeling me, so I just blindly keep on going. Despite not knowing if anyone can hear me.

UNDRESSED

SHE'S NOT THERE

My Mom never called me
On Thanksgiving

I know she is suffering
I know she is forgetful
I know she is alone

Yet when I call her

She's not there.

Commentary: After my Dad died everything changed. My mom became a ghost, and I spent Thanksgiving alone. I'm not feeling sorry for myself, I am just sorry for everything.

Erica Loberg

YOU SAID I THREW YOU OUT

You said I threw you out
Like I was the one in the wrong

You said you loved me
Like I was the only one

You said a lot
That I try to forget.

Commentary: I am good at three things in life. Writing, blowjobs and dancing. That's it. If I could do life over again, I might have been a dancer but, I don't have the body for that so when I found out my boyfriend was going to take his ex-girlfriend dancing, I lost my shit. He never took me dancing in all the years we were together. He liked my writing, he enjoyed my blow jobs, so why didn't he ever take me dancing?

UNDRESSED

WITHOUT A HOME

I wander the streets
Alone
Among the muck
Of dying life
Of naked hairs
Of lost minds.

And wonder how do people make it
Without a home
And how do people with a home want to move someone
Without a home?

Commentary: I have lived in DTLA for almost ten years. People think with all the construction and migration of rich people who can't afford the Westside anymore, that the homeless population will just disappear. Just go away. Ah, no. The same sad lives walk the same deadly streets despite all that people do to try and rid the world of an eye soar. These are people ok.

Erica Loberg

ROCK OUT WITH YOUR COCK OUT

Sometimes it's worrisome
That my mom is so afraid
Of my craziness….

Like I wild out
Ok

Maybe I don't simmer in
Depression
All day

But rock out with my cock out.

Commentary: Practically every time I come across a little too excited, or have rushed language, I get the same old response from my Mom, "Are you taking your meds?" I know she means well but it's annoying cause I am the most med compliant person I've ever met, and it's as if she freaks out with the idea of me off of my medication. I realize she raised hypo manic child, which must have been challenging, but I'm not manic anymore. And even if I were, so what. Can't I just wild out sometimes like normal people?

UNDRESSED

TWICE, FRANKLY

First I fucked him
Twice

Then I puked
Twice

Wait….

One happened
Then the other happened
Then one happened again
Then the other happened again

Who fucks someone and pukes then
Fucks again

Both of us frankly.

Commentary: I spent two years in therapy trying to get over my ex-boyfriend, and managed to block him for six whole months then, over the holidays, I unblocked him and next thing I know we are having sex. Yes, I was drunk and had too much tequila but, I also was so disgusted with myself that I threw up. I literally got up and puked, went back to bed, and screwed him again, then puked again. Note to self: stay away from toxic people and if you puke pay attention cause you are disgusted with yourself, as you should be.

Erica Loberg

THE "NUKE" AKA THE NUCLEAR DICK OFF

I gotta better nuke
I gotta bigger nuke

Mine is better
Mine is bigger

Bigger or Better...

If Jung-un has a better dick
And Trump has a bigger dick...?
That's a rough call

On who would press
The dick off button.

Both are fat
Both have fat in their dick

No one wants a piece of that
No one wants a nuclear war
Cause your dick is not a nuke

So stop having a dick off.

Commentary: This poem is inspired by President Trump when he gave a speech on nuclear war which compared his nuke button to North Korea. So ridiculous.

UNDRESSED

CRUNCH

I didn't think I had crunches in my mouth
When I kissed you

I did.

Commentary: I'm so fat that I eat ice cream and go straight to bed, usually I do the whole face cleaning, brushing of the teeth, etc. And, of course this one time I eat ice cream with almonds in it my booty call drops by and I find myself kissing him and moving the crunches in my mouth away from his tongue so he doesn't know. Jesus Erica, really?

Erica Loberg

ANOTHER TOMORROW

You said you'd call me tomorrow
That was after you fucked me

Tomorrow became
Another tomorrow
Then the next tomorrow
Than another tomorrow

Fuck and flight
Hit it and quit it
Ding Dong Ditch Dick

Why say you'll call me tomorrow
When it's just

Another tomorrow.

Commentary: I am a sucker for guys that do drive by shootings in the middle of the night. My ex-boyfriend would show up and we'd have sex and he'd say he'd call me the next day and then nothing. The sad part is it happened to me more than once, and somehow I couldn't seem to free myself from being used and abused by a lying sack of shit. Time to reenter therapy I suppose.

UNDRESSED

THIRD EYE BLIND

I have skin cancer on my face
Damn smack in the middle of my forehead

I call it my third eye blind

My Father died of cancer
In his lungs, in his neck, in his stomach

I'd rather have cancer on the outside
Then on the inside

And get proper treatment

And not die.

Commentary: I grew up playing outdoors a lot: volleyball, tennis, skiing, sailing, surfing all the time, with zero sunscreen. I literally would become a fried tomato. But, now I am paying the consequences of that with skin cancer, which I get treated for every few months. It's funny cause I had it on my face for years, and didn't do anything about it. Then my sister had cancer on her hairline so I thought maybe I should get it checked out. My Dad had cancer for three months and never saw a Doctor. Eric and Erica. Like father like daughter. I learned that denial runs deep in my family, cause who has cancer and doesn't get it checked out??

Erica Loberg

YOU LIE

You lie and lie and lie and lie and lie and lie and lie and lie
And

I'm still here.

Commentary: It is pathetic, and sad, that I was in a relationship with a sociopath for years, and dealt with so many lies that I had to stop and think, who really is the problem here? ME!

UNDRESSED

WHAT'S NEXT

Politics meets
Reality TV meets
Donald trump meets
The Apprentice meets
Omarosa meets
Celebrity Big Brother meets
Fake news meets
Florida student "actor"

Who's watching?

What's next?

Commentary: I wrote this poem when America at the time was a total mess. It's as if our culture was so celebrity driven to the point that we appointed a "reality star" aka Donald Trump to be President. Once he was inaugurated he hired Omarosa, who was one of his finalists on Trumps reality show *Celebrity Apprentice*. After a year in office, she was removed from the white house, and the next thing you know she was on the new *Celebrity Big Brother*. On top of that, whenever there was news that reflected negatively on Trump, he would call it "fake news." And believe it or not, the most ridiculous thing that occurred was when there was a high school shooting in Florida that killed 17 students, and there was a movement to monitor gun control and students that stood up to the white house, and modern day politics, on this matter were called "actors." It begged the question, who is watching this shit, and what the hell is going to happen next?

Erica Loberg

I'M NOT RACIST

"I'm not racist."
My mom said.

"I just prefer white people."

"I'm not racist."
I said.

"I just prefer black people."

Commentary: My Mom has never flat out said she was racist, but, she also has never minced words and so, yes, she prefers white people. I have always appreciated her honesty, despite the racism behind it. This comment was made at a time when she had caregivers around the clock and "preferred" white caregivers over black caregivers. She comes from a different generation, as do I and yes, if I were pressed to make a decision I might say I prefer black people. But I don't consider myself racist. And for whatever reason, it has been my experience that black people better get my sense of humor more so than white people. What I like about this poem is it is more of a statement of two different generations but in my opinion, I think people would be offended by my mother's statement and less offended my mine, which is not fair, but that's the world we live in.

UNDRESSED

THE BLOCK

I've been around the block
Girl, you've built a city within a city.

Commentary: I am a member of the Los Angeles Athletic Club, and one of the servers there knows me for being open about sex talk which is the root of his around the block statement. Or maybe I am just honest among the khaki and polo shirts running around pretending.

Erica Loberg

WHEN I'M ON TOP

Is your dick
Denting my insides?

Knocking on the door of
My insides?

When I'm on top?

Commentary: This poem more or less describes what sex feels like for me on my insides when I am having sex on top.

UNDRESSED

OVER HIM

I guess the only way to tell if you are over a dick
Is to suck it

It might not be that big as you thought
Or unique

It's just a dick

That's when you know you are

Over him.

Commentary: I talked earlier about the BJ Club and committing so, if you're not willing to commit to a BJ you're flat out not into it and over him. It's a good barometer of where you're at with your love.

Erica Loberg

HARSH

"I don't want to talk to her, ever."

it's not the first time
i've heard it and
certainly not the last

"I'm done talking with her."

but, to hear it from your
mother
and your
sister

and for it to be real

is harsh.

Comment: When my father died, my family fell apart. My mother had to be conserved, and her conservator manipulated her to believe she should never speak with her family members anymore. And my sister married a control freak terrorist that also brainwashed her to pretty much disown me. So, I more or less lost my dad, my mom, and my sister, and was left with just me. It was harsh.

UNDRESSED

I LICKED THE INSIDE OF MY CUP

I licked the inside of my cup
of coffee
that I got at the
coffee bean

after pouring an-okay amount of
vanilla power
all over
the top

i licked the inside of my cup.

I sat across a gangster
from East LA

that knew how to make change
as in coin
off of... whatever she was dealing at the time
Cocaine
Weed
Crack
Crup....

but she didn't know how to lip the inside of her cup.

Commentary: I once worked doing homeless outreach for the mentally ill. It was a dumping ground for people that were being disciplined by the government. Most of my co-workers had a colorful past, and came from different walks of life. One of my co-workers was a Chola from East Los Angeles. She had a criminal past, had done time in jail, and was a force to not be reckoned with. When I first met her she was racist against white people. I was the "white girl from the Westside," where as she was, "a Latina from the East side." Slowly we became friends, despite the racist undertones. When we were partners, we would drive around LA County to outreach homeless people, and often times she would sip beer out of a straw, while blasting her hip hop music. On one occasion we stopped for coffee. I like my ice coffee with some half and half and to top it off with that vanilla sugar powder, so, by the time I finish it, some of the sugar would be left on the inside of the cup. This one particular time I saw her watch me lick the sugar around the inside of my cup and saw her eyes wide open like she just discovered hot sauce for a burrito. She was baffled by the fact that she never knew of the sugar lip trick, despite all her tricks, and every time since she would lick the shit out of the inside of the cup with pleasant pleasure. You're welcome girl!

UNDRESSED

IT WAS AN ASPHALT BLOOD BATH

they used to just roll bodies out
of cars
onto the street

gangs would go
bang bang

then drop off dead gangers
outside of

Martin Luther King Jr. Hospital

so they had to close it

it was an asphalt blood bath.

Commentary: I once worked in an acute psychiatric ward at Augustus Hawkins in Compton, CA. It was adjacent to MLK Jr. Hospital and while I was there I learned it was shut down years ago due to gangs. If a gang member was shot, in order to ensure the rest of the gang wouldn't get in trouble they would just drop them off outside the ER and they would bleed to death on the sidewalk. It recently reopened, and now I work with clients that go there, and they don't get the best mental health services, so, maybe it will be closed at some point again.

Erica Loberg

SHE CHOPPED OFF HER TITS, OK!

I was talking to a friend yesterday about the "me too"
Movement
She said she didn't really know much about it.

I asked her if she had ever been sexually harassed
She said yes.

She was harassed at her first job
When she was seventeen-years-old.

I asked how she responded
She said she thought if she got a boob reduction

Her boss would stop staring at her chest, so...

SHE CHOPPED OFF HER TITS, OK!

Commentary: My co-worker was a size double D and, at her first job she experienced sexual harassment and so she decided to get a breast reduction. I was shocked when she told me. Not so much that she had a breast reduction, but she said it like it was no big deal and never really thought about it before. In her mind the sexual harassment meant she needed to adjust her body versus putting blame on the harasser. The power of sexual harassment on young women marks them for life, literally.

UNDRESSED

AMAZON IS FOR POOR PEOPLE

It says
Best seller
Amazon selected choice!

Amazon tricked me into becoming a prime member
I guess I selected a trial run for a week
And then became a prime member with zero notice
And was billed 100 dollars

They basically unasked me into the prime zone
So now I am buying more then I would
On Amazon.

My psychiatrist has this light
outside his office
that says
please hit the LED light when you arrive

I didn't know what LED meant
he was dumbfound when I asked him, and he tried to explain it to me
with my blank face

So, I ordered an LED light
Which was an Amazon top rated light
It arrived and

It was a light you would use in a lab for rats

WTF

Then I ordered sheets based on
Amazons recommendations
and got sheets that
felt like I was
in a hospital bed.

Amazon is for poor people

Erica Loberg

I don't want to sleep in hospital bed sheets
and write with a florist rat light above me.

Commentary: The best line in this poem that says it all which happens to be in the middle is, "So they unasked me into the prime zone".

UNDRESSED

THE SIMPSON EFFECT

there is wisdom in age
there is wisdom in color

he runs the psychiatric unit at
USC

he is tall, black, and gave me the advice of
a lifetime

whenever you come across a decision
give it 48 hours

take out a piece of paper
and write down what you want to do
or say

walk away
then come back

it has saved me from
many impulsive moments
many misunderstood times
many party fouls and regrets

I call it

The Simpson Effect

Commentary: This poem is dedicated to Dr. Simpson who spends his days working in a psych ward treating the mentally ill at Augustus Hawkins Hospital in Compton, CA.

Erica Loberg

THE HOT SEAT

Oh thank God
Matt Lauer
Is sizzling on the hot seat

That I had to roast on
Yesterday.

Fhewwww.

Does that mean I'm off the hot seat...?

Ah....no

Your dumb ass will always leave a mark
On

The hot seat.

Commentary: This poem is dedicated to all the sexual predators out there that were in the news during the "me too" movement. When the movement started it was as if every week another predator was exposed. This poem starts with the voice of one of the predators being thankful that someone else was on the hot seat but, no, you're not, and your actions will always leave a stain.

UNDRESSED

THE AMERICAN WAY

Thank you Trump!

Yes! Finally there is a surge of
Hell-no
No you didn't
That bubbled beneath the surface of
Freedom

The American way.

Supposedly depends on your America.

Thank you Donald Trump
For making misogyny
A locker room
Buzz word

You lit the match to those
At the mercy of
"Locker room"
Talk.

Would we be here in an outpour of women
Stepping forth if
T-Rex didn't start the fire
By making
misogamy,
sexual harassment, and,
sexual assault

The American Way

THANK YOU DONALD TRUMP!

Commentary: I think Trump had a hand in starting the "me too" movement cause America elected a President that had a history of sexual assault, yet, he was still put in office. I believe this started a silent rumble among women that at one point exploded and exposed every sucker out there.

Erica Loberg

SHAKIN' IN YOUR F'IN BOOTS

I wonder how many men
Are shaking in their boots right now?

Knowing that all these other men
Are forced to deal with the truth

That they assaulted women.

Are they paying off their victims
Like Bill Cosby?
(television)

Are they blaming God
Like Bill O'Reilly ?
(media)

Are they apologizing
Like George Bush?
(politics)

Are they denying
Like Harvey Weinstein?
(film)

Are they trying to quietly disappear
Like Mark Halperin?
(news)

Well, they are from all over the place
And they are doing all of it so...

What exactly are you doing right now...?

Shaking in your F'in boots.

Commentary: I can't imagine being a sexual predator at this time when one by one all types of people in the media were being exposed. Imagine going to work and living in fear that if you had a history of abuse, you might be the next one on the chopping block. Good, bring it.

UNDRESSED

I NEED SOME FRESH AIR

He was my professor in college
He was worldly known, scholastic, prestigious, astute

I was his student
I was nineteen, sharp, eager, curious, enthusiastic

I liked him
But not like that

He liked me
But like that

I rode the elevator with him once
He complimented my tan skin

I was stuck in an elevator
I could take a compliment

Then later that afternoon
I received an email

"I need some fresh air."

Whatever *that* means…..

Commentary: When I started out as am English major I was told I had no business being an English major, let alone a writer. But, by the time senior year came around I was at the top of my class. This poem is about one of my Professors that taught a seminar on Shakespeare, and developed a thing for me. I was too naïve at the time to handle such a thing and when I got that text I didn't respond. Then at the end of the seminar he had a party at his apartment in New York. When I arrived everyone was drinking wine out of plastic cups but for me he took out a glass and poured me some fine wine. I'll take it, thanks.

Erica Loberg

THE SECUTIRY GUARD

I was at the pool
Late night

I do not see a difference
Between a bra and underwear
And a bathing suit.

So wore my bra and underwear

In the pool.

When my clothes were taken
I was left with flip flops
And my bra and underwear.

When the security guard came up to
Close the pool
I realized
I was going to take my ass home
In a bra and underwear
Which I did

I rode that elevator home
Dripping water off my tits
and chilling flip flops
with the security guard

A few days later
I walked by that same
security guard
knowing he saw me
being awesome

I went to CVS to get some tampons
And a twix
And walked back into
my building and

UNDRESSED

dropped off the twix
To the security guard

A few hours later
I was conducting my usual
Checking out the neighborhood
With my binoculars
Perusing the scene
from my window

And saw him

My security guard
Walking
With his suspenders
And twix in hand
and he stepped onto a bus

On his way home.

Commentary: My loft building in Downtown LA always seemed to have a rotating door of doormen. I developed a soft spot for this particular doorman, cause he never made me feel embarrassed about practically being naked and ashamed that my clothes were stolen. Sometimes he would make a comment if I didn't say hello or goodbye when I entered and exited the building. Like it hurt his feelings or something. It's hard to be on all the time but seeing him from my window walk home developed more compassion in me, and moving forward I made an effort to be extra nice going in and out of my building

Erica Loberg
GYNOCOLOGIST APPOINTMENT

When was your last period?
I guess the last time I

Prayed for it.

Commentary: Ah… I have had unprotected sex with my ex for yearssss. We used the rhythm method, and every freaking time I would stress about getting pregnant and prayed that I would get my period every month. He refused to wear condoms, and I didn't want to be on the pill but, why would I put myself through the stress and anxiety praying for my period every month? I did.

UNDRESSED

MY DICK

All I have left is my package, right now

I can dance with my thicker legs
And flubber on my stomach
But when I rock my hips up and down
With my rod

It is there.

It doesn't age
Or fall
Or get fat

I wonder if a women's
Vagina lips fall
Does the skin get fat, and gravity pulls it down?

I don't know
I'm just glad I have

My Dick.

Commentary: I wrote this poem from a male's perspective. I like writing from a male's point of view from time to time. I'm pretty sure at this point in my life I can say I have penis envy. Although I love being a woman, I think it is easier physically to be a man when it comes to anatomy. Anyway, I had a gay friend that told me at some point in life my vagina lips would drop. And when I would gain weight, I swear I felt like my lips would get fatter. It didn't seem fair that a dick stays the same. But later I learned that men's balls drop sometime around 50 so, no one is free from the aging of the private parts.

Erica Loberg

CILANTRO

I have a pet mosquito
His name is Cilantro

Every night at 3 am
He buzzes in my ear

I used to slap at my face
In the dark
But would always
Miss him

He drove me crazy.

Then I would have repellant spray
Like a gun in a holster
By my bed
Ready to go
And would
Spray my arms and neck
In the middle of the night
And sit
And wait
To hear him.

And he would come
I could see my Fat Cat
Swat at the air
So I knew he was around

He was a seasonal pet
I don't know where he lived
In my place
But I've known him for a couple years

Last night was the first night I slept
In weeks
Without my 3 am wake up call

From Cilantro

UNDRESSED

I thought I would be thrilled
But I woke up feeling empty
And wondering

Where did my little Cilantro go?

Commentary: I live in a loft filled with plants, like my place is a jungle, so, it's no wonder with water around I would have a mosquito problem. Cilantro would come and visits a certain time of year, and would drive me crazy. Eventually I bought one of those repellant bracelets and wore it on both my arms and ankles, and I remember the next time he tried to strike he was zapped away. Gotta bitch!

Erica Loberg

THERAPY

It's like buyers regret.

You cancel your therapy session
Then feel bad about it
Then want to re-schedule it
Then worry about feeling anxious about it.

It's like two types of stress
Both rooted in the same thing

Therapy.

Commentary: I swear to God making any commitment to plans is merely impossible for me, however, therapy is something I forced on myself and making and keeping that appointment would cause so much anxiety for me that eventually I had to quit.

UNDRESSED

OH MY HOLY COCKROACH

I decided to get my nails done
Toes that is

Aw
Nice
Refreshing
Chill

Listening to the Red Hot Chili Peppers
On my headphones
And then
A baby walker

A roach
Crawls on my chair

In a nail salon?
The hygiene center of America?

I flicked it
Off the chair
Into the bubbled water
That previously soaked my feet

My toe lady looked over
Into the water

The roach was slowly drowning to its death

Don't worry about it
I said
It's all good

And she polished my toes.

Commentary: So, here's what I learned about this experience. Not only did I pay for the pedicure and not say a word to the owner, I ended up paying double for the tip, why? Cause I felt bad for the salon, and the woman having to see the roach? *I* felt guilty? That's when I looked into co-dependency issues, and things started to change in my life. All due to a cockroach.

UNDRESSED

TO YOUR LOVE

A sweet serenity
A quiet call

To your love

Not cause it's a new year
But cause it's
You

A silent call

To your love.

Commentary: I'm not sure if this is a poem about positive or negative love cause it seems like it's a celebration of love but making it quiet seems sad to me.

Erica Loberg

DID YOUR DICK FALL OFF IN THE MIDDLED OF THE NIGHT?

Sometimes artists take themselves
too seriously
I watch the "With or Without You"
Video

And Bono takes himself
so seriously
As he should

I guess he has earned it
Or was just always like that

It's him.

So when people say....
Whatever they are going to say
Or not....

Or show their look away
from serious

Of me.

I shouldn't be surprised

Did your dick fall off in the middle of the night?

Commentary: Sometimes I can say some random things out of nowhere, and people will look at me funny. One day I walked out of therapy and was catching up with the security guard outside the building when this guy stopped us on the street. He looked confused. He was lost and needed directions. So when the man approached us asking for directions, the security guard tried to steer him in the right direction. He still looked confused and for whatever reason, I interjected and said, "Did your dick fall off in the middle of the night?" You should have seen their faces. Bono can do and say whatever he wants so why can't I? Ok, I'm not a rock star, but still.

UNDRESSED

MERRY HINDU

"We're going to have to take a biopsy of that spot on your forehead."
"Okayyyy. Like today, now?"
"Do you want to wait until after Christmas, cause it will be sore."
"And you mean I'll have to wear a Band-Aid across my face."
"Yes."
"Cut away, I'm converting to Hinduism after this."

Commentary: I've had cancer on my face in the middle of my forehead for a long time. Initially, I would get it frozen every few months, which really wasn't working. When my Father died I lost my PPO insurance, and had to switch to an HMO, and so all my Doctors had to change. When I went to this new dermatologist she suggested we do a biopsy to check for malignant cancer. When she did the biopsy it was around Christmas time and I think she was worried about me looking bad around the family. I didn't care. I was planning on spending Christmas alone so made a joke about it. It came back benign but, it's still there to this day.

Erica Loberg

JUSTICE

not only was Axel
wearing his
undies
at the piano

he had white socks
on his feet.

And i'm not considered
a rockstar for walking around
half naked
in
flip flops?

Commentary: Guns N Roses is my favorite rock band. This poem is inspired by a video of them performing *November Rain* in Tokyo in 1991. For the majority of the show he had on tittie whities which I found hilarious. I'm a quasi-nudist. I hate feeling confined, so, when I am home I sport a shirt and underwear, with my flip flops. Even if I have company I do it. If Axel can do it in front of thousands of people why can't I?

UNDRESSED

THE NERVOUS BREAKDOWN

My mind swims in the middle of the night
It's like a live rollercoaster in my brain
Sometimes I have to crawl on all fours to get to the bathroom
I know this is bad
I knew this was coming
And I am at a loss of words on what to do
Or how to stop it

The nervous breakdown.

Commentary: The breakdown list is so long and horrific it is almost impossible to comment on the source of this poem. My mom is conserved by a crook that is taking all her money, all my inheritance, all the family assets, all the life out of her, and me, and I have been standing strong trying to remove him but he keeps winning. Now the FBI are involved for his white collar crimes, and I pray they bring him to justice before I end up not walking on all fours to take a piss in the middle of the night but end up flat on the ground in a full blown meltdown.

Erica Loberg

JUST WRONG

...I thought it was about
life liberty and the pursuit of happiness

it meaning the flag, and the song

i thought the flag was a sign of freedom
of self expression

and individualism among a group of
stars like me, or not

but I could stand up
or sit down
or spin

cause freedom is a must
not a choice

but freedom's not a choice
anymore

ah.. the irony

you can't kneel to a flag
or a song of liberty

cause your freedoms are removed

then what's it all about, really?

...ah... not irony, just wrong.

Commentary: This poem is dedicated to the players in the NFL that are no longer allowed to kneel during the anthem due to fascistic behavior imposed by our current government.

UNDRESSED

MAN

Don't dude me
Or "man" me
Your dick has been inside me
So
Unless your gay
Don' t dude me.

Man

Commentary: I can not stand it when a guy calls me dude cause that means he is not into you like that, ok.

Erica Loberg

SIMPLE

Republicans are dicks
Democrats are vaginas

Read into it what you want
But

It's that simple.

Commentary: If there were to be a street fight between Republicans and Democrats, the Republicans would show up with guns, and the Democrats would show up with knives. Michelle Obama said, "They go low, we go high." How about they go low, we go lower. I think that if the Democrats want to gain any momentum, or hold any power or authority, they need to grow some brass balls, and tell the Republicans to suck my freckled dick, ok!

UNDRESSED

THE TEAM....?

I constantly feel like I take one
For the team

But,

I'm the only one on it....

Commentary: I decided to end *Undressed* with this poem cause I have found a pattern in my life that has made it hard to live a normal life. I fight a lot of good fights that no one seems to want to take on. I'm like a warrior that looks around, and sees fallen soldiers all around me. I stand up for the underdog, the silenced ones, the people that walk alone in life, and face injustices. You are not alone, and I'll keep up the fight.

www.ingramcontent.com/pod-product-compliance
Ingram Content Group UK Ltd.
Pitfield, Milton Keynes, MK11 3LW, UK
UKHW041412180426
11947UKWH00007B/90